The Kwara'ae

The Solomon Islanders are a people of many i...
Kwara'ae live on Malaita, the most populous of the many islands.

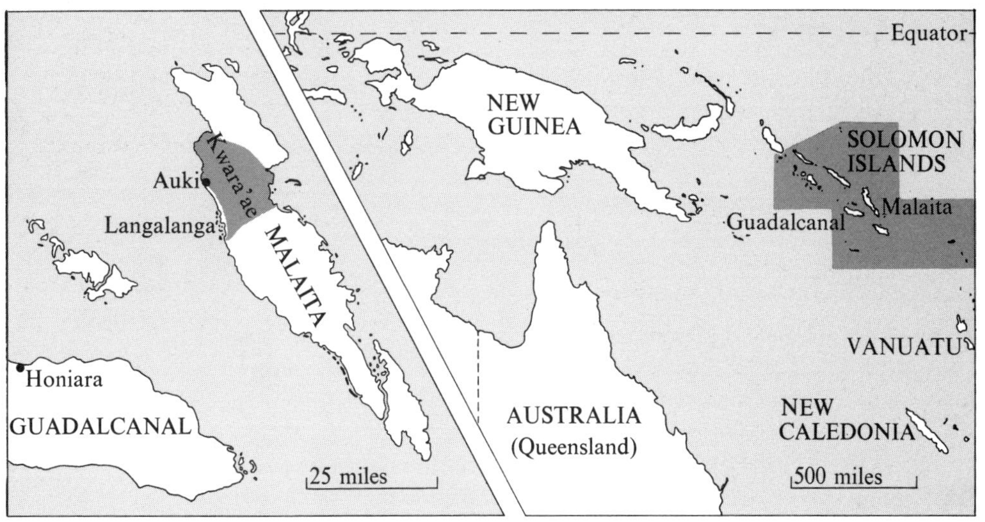

Map of Malaita and the Solomon Islands in the Southwest Pacific.

The Kwara'ae people tell the story of how their ancestors first came to Malaita, the mountainous forested island which is their home. Long ago, perhaps twenty generations past, a man sailed from Asia with his wife and family. He landed first on the neighbouring island of Guadalcanal, then crossed to the west coast of Malaita. He lived in one place after another, guided on his way by a magical staff which the Kwara'ae still keep today. Eventually it led him to a place in the hills in the middle of the island where he settled and where he built a great shrine called Siele. Here his descendants sacrificed pigs to him after his death, in the way that Kwara'ae have worshipped their dead ancestors ever since. This man brought with him all the rules of respect for the ancestors, for sacred things, for property and for persons which were the basis of the traditional Kwara'ae way of life, their 'custom' as they call it today. This custom way of life was faithfully handed down over the generations as his descendants spread out over the land which now belongs to the Kwara'ae people.

Few Kwara'ae follow this way of life strictly today. Like other peoples around the world they have had to adapt themselves to many changes since the colonial powers of Europe took over their lands. For more than a century men have been taking temporary jobs for European businesses operating in the Pacific, and many years ago most Kwara'ae abandoned their ancestors to become Christians. Nonetheless their custom is remembered and plays an important part in modern life.

Kwara'ae is only one of twelve different languages and dialects spoken on the island of Malaita, but the twelve and a half thousand Kwara'ae speakers are the largest language group not only on Malaita but in the whole of the Solomon Islands. In many ways all Malaitans share a similar

(*Left*) A dancer in fine ornaments with leg rattles and a hornbill baton.

(*Cover*) Timi Ko'oliu, a senior priest among the few Kwara'ae who still worship their ancestors.

way of life. Like other Solomon Islanders, most are farmers, and their traditional lifestyle depends above all else on their land, inherited from the ancestors they worshipped.

Ancestors and land

The Kwara'ae explain how, from the time of the first settlers, elder sons usually took charge of their fathers' land. They acted as priests, sacrificing pigs to their ancestors at shrines like Siele where the skulls and other relics of the dead were kept. Over the generations some men would leave their forefathers' lands to settle new districts, cutting clearings in the virgin forests to build their small hamlets and make gardens for their crops. Their sons and grandsons in turn inherited the land they had claimed and sacrificed to them in shrines where they had lived and died. As time went on the whole of Kwara'ae became dotted with these shrines, whose buildings and altars were concealed in stands of tall trees on the ridges and hilltops. They mark the territories established by the early settlers and inherited ever since by groups descended from them in the male line.

However, many of the people living in these territories today are descended, often many generations back, from women of the group which owns the land. People may use the land of their mother's line, too, and in the past they would also sacrifice to its ancestors. If land were given to them they might establish shrines there for the ancestors of their own line, and pass the land on to their descendants, but otherwise they are more or less guests of the original owners of the land. Deciding to whom a piece of land belongs and who is allowed to farm it can become very complicated. Every piece of land belongs to someone, and people still farm it because the ancestors they used to worship lived there before them.

Making a living

Today Kwara'ae can earn money to buy manufactured goods and imported food, but few people depend on wages alone or 'live by money' as they say. Most still make their living largely by growing their own food on their ancestral lands much as they have for centuries past.

The land itself, like other islands in this part of the world, is covered with thick forest, fast growing in the tropical heat, and year-round heavy rainfall. Gardens are made by cutting and burning a clearing in the forest growth on suitable land, often on steep hillsides as there is little level ground. Crops are planted as cuttings in holes made by thrusting a heavy stick between the roots and stones, and the gardens are neatly laid out with poles marking different plots. After a year or two the forest is allowed to regrow, letting the land regenerate for future years. In the past the main crops were yam and taro tubers. Today sweet potatoes are more important and many more kinds of food are grown: coconuts, greens, bananas, sugar cane, cassava among others. Besides all these, nuts are gathered in the forest and there are various wild fruits and seeds, as well as birds and other small creatures

A taro garden. The tops of plants already harvested are replanted on new ground.

The east coast of Malaita, viewed from one of the small islands of the 'saltwater' people.

which can be eaten. Chickens and pigs are kept in the villages, but meat is eaten only at feasts or special occasions. The Kwara'ae also obtain fish in weekly markets on the coast where they trade their garden produce with people living on the small offshore islands. Only these 'saltwater' people make a living from the sea, and their way of life, as well as their language, is rather different from that of the mainland 'bush' people.

In the past the farming way of life was much the same for everyone. All men and women learned the same basic skills to provide the necessities of life and everyone shared a similar standard of living. In many ways this is still true today, but now those who earn money can pay for European material comforts which were unavailable before. However, although men began to work for wages in the last century, until recently few earned enough to make much difference to their life at home. At first the most important goods they obtained were steel tools, which proved much more efficient than the old stone ones for clearing gardens and woodworking.

Originally, like the more old-fashioned people today, everyone lived in small hamlets of one or two families in scattered forest clearings, linked by the steep and slippery narrow paths which are still the main routes through most of the area. They built low houses walled with bamboo and thatched with leaves, where they cooked and slept on the earth floors. Domestic arrangements were simple: food was prepared with shell knives and cooked in bamboo tubes roasted on the fire, or steamed, covered with leaves, on hot stones. Vegetables were mashed in wooden bowls to make puddings and water was fetched in bamboo bottles. Useful objects were made from forest products: plaited baskets and bags from leaves or shredded bark, belts and straps from cane, and tools, weapons and utensils carved from wood. Most people now build more elaborate houses in larger villages and use manufactured goods from cooking pots and oil lamps to transistor radios, but they still rely on these old skills to make many of the things which are needed from day to day.

(*Above right*) Buildings like this are used as kitchens and living quarters: today most Kwara'ae build their private sleeping houses on stilts.

(*Below right*) Inside a small kitchen a woman prepares taro with her shell knife.

4

Wealth and leadership

In the past individuals who were more prosperous and successful than others had few material comforts which were not available to all. However, prosperity had other rewards, for by working hard and managing his resources carefully a man could gain respect and influence in his community. This was done by building up wealth in the strings of shell beads which were used for the exchanges of gifts so important in Kwara'ae community life. This 'shell money' is made by the saltwater people on the west coast of Malaita or by bush people in the southern part of the island. It is valuable because so much work is involved in grinding and drilling the beads, and formerly it could be exchanged for almost anything which today can be bought and sold for Solomon Island dollars. Shell money could be earned by selling garden produce, pigs or craftwork and sometimes by working for others, but if large amounts were needed it had to be borrowed. To get married a man had to give many strings of money as 'bridewealth' to his wife's family, who would provide pigs and vegetables for the wedding feast. Christians now limit this gift to five sets of strings, worth about $100 each, but in the past four or even six times this amount might be required. By helping his relatives with shell money at times like this a shrewd man could put many people in his debt and be sure of similar assistance when he needed it himself. In this way he could raise greater quantities of shell money than he actually owned at any one time. Someone who could give more than his neighbours when helping others or contribut-

(*Above left*) Paramount Chief Rofate'e with shell money made by the 'saltwater' people of Langalanga (see map p.1).

(*Above*) the beads, strung in a unit of ten strings.

6

ing to feasts became indispensable to his local community. He could encourage his relatives to live and work with him, and adopt children to swell the workforce of his family. Men like this, involved in everyones' business, were treated with respect and their advice was taken seriously. Although they had no way of forcing obedience, they were nonetheless the leaders on whom the community's welfare depended.

The living and the dead

From the Kwara'ae point of view, however, welfare and prosperity depended not only on the efforts of the living but also on the goodwill of the dead ancestors who had owned the land before them. The ancestors watched over their descendants using their power to protect and aid them, or to punish them if they did wrong. It was they who made the gardens and pigs thrive, who brought health, wealth and good fortune. In return they expected to share in the prosperity of the living, to receive token offerings of crops from a new garden, of shell money, and, on important occasions, sacrifices of pigs.

The responsibility for keeping people on good terms with their ancestors lay with the senior man of each small group of brothers, fathers and adult sons who lived and worked together on the land they shared. As their priest this man carried out their sacrifices at the shrines of the ancestors they shared in the male line. It was he who memorised the lists of ancestors going back to the earliest times, which was essential not only to the rituals but to establish ownership of the land. A priest was supposed to be descended through a line of eldest sons from the ancestor who first claimed

Pork for a feast, cooked on the hot stones at the right, is cut into strips to give to relatives and neighbours.

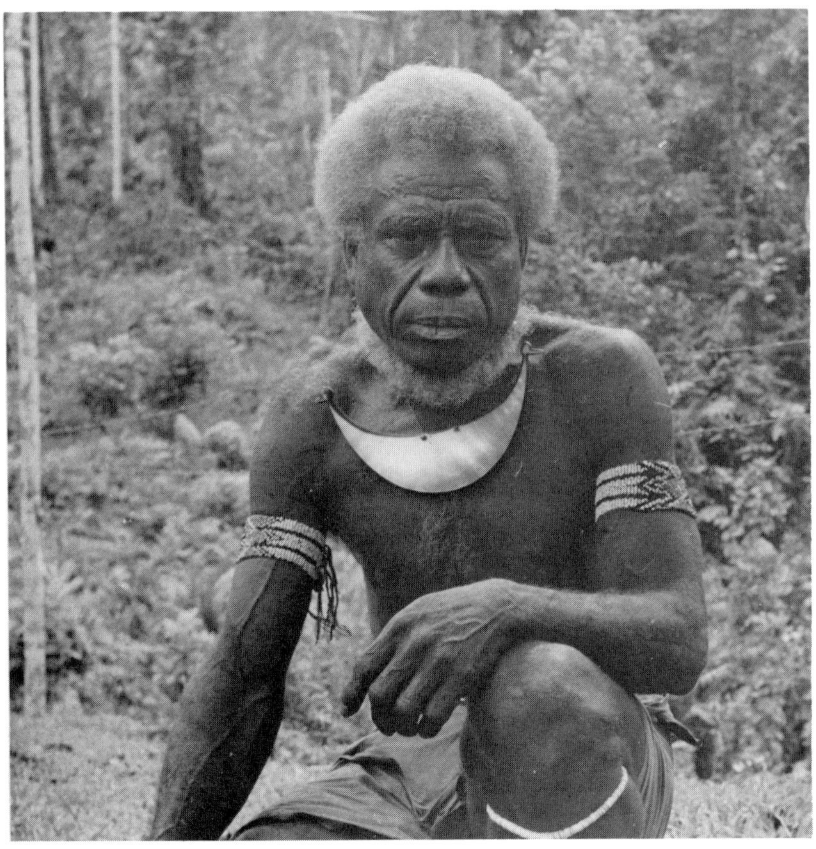

Maeorora, a priest, dressed in traditional ornaments: a pearl-shell pendant, shell bead armbands and garters.

this land, and he was in charge of the land and its shrines. Priests of more ancient shrines were senior to the others, being responsible for the powerful ancestors shared and worshipped by a number of these local groups, and most respected of all were the priests of major shrines like Siele, where the first ancestor or his sons were worshipped. In practice, of course, the eldest sons of senior lines were not always best suited to these positions and others often came forward, perhaps because their ancestors had chosen them in dreams. The responsibilities involved helped senior priests become influential leaders among their people.

Under the leadership of their priests groups of men organised big sacrificial feasts for all the ancestors in the male line from whom they inherited their land. Depending on the number of men involved and the importance of the shrine anything up to a hundred pigs might be sacrificed at one time. The ancestors only consumed the spirits of the pigs. The meat would be shared among all the men descended from them including those descended from women of their line, whose own ancestral lands lay elsewhere. Since almost everyone in a district was related in some way or other, however many generations back, these feasts were big social occasions in which many people took part. Men dressed up in their best ornaments: shells and fancy combs in their hair, carved shell pendants, shell bead armbands, cane belts and other fine objects, decorated with bright leaves. There were dances with music from panpipes and rattles, and, of course, there was the luxury of meat and other fine food.

These feasts were held every few years whenever the ancestors saw that enough full-grown pigs were ready and instructed the priest in his dreams. They were important occasions, not only because they gave people the chance to show their wealth and generosity to their neighbours, but because they were essential for the goodwill of the ancestors, on which everyone's lives depended. The rituals which the priests conducted to benefit from the ancestors' power were very sacred and required the observance of strict rules by everyone involved. For many days before the feast no-one should create any disturbance or attend marriages, funerals or other social occasions.

The rules of good living

However, it took more than occasional feasts to keep the ancestors happy, for they were concerned above all that their descendants led correct lives according to the rules brought by the first ancestors. These rules were based on the idea that the important things in life had to be treated with special care and respect and protected from abuse: they were *tambu*. In their different ways persons, homes, gardens and property were all *tambu*. Most *tambu* of all were the ancestors, their shrines and everything to do with their worship, including the adult men who shared in the sacrifices and, of course, the priests who performed them. Men and the ancestors had to be protected in particular from the wrong kind of contact with women, who were regarded as unclean, especially during their monthly periods and after childbirth. At these times women had to seclude themselves in a special house outside the hamlet, downhill so that their unclean influence

A dance of the kind performed at sacrificial feasts, with music from panpipes and rattles (as in the picture opposite page 1).

would not drift around the houses and defile their menfolk. Because this defilement always flowed downward, men were protected from day to day by making sure that women never stepped over them, bathed upstream from them or went above them or their possessions in any way. Women used the downhill side of the house for their domestic work and the special houses where men gathered to talk or where priests kept sacred relics of their ancestors, were always uphill and forbidden to women. Women could not enter shrines or eat sacrificial meat. The ancestors were angered by anyone breaking these rules, even accidentally. If a woman defiled men or sacred things, even if smoke from the cooking fire she used during her monthly period drifted over a shrine, they were likely to punish their descendants, the people who were defiled by the mistake.

When someone became ill it was at once suspected that an ancestor was offended for some reason, and was demanding a pig from them. It was for the priests to discover which ancestors were responsible, and they sacrificed and cooked the pigs. Besides defilement by women, the ancestors punished many other faults in the same way: quarrels and misbehaviour which spoilt the harmony of the family group, or making the village or gardens dirty and untidy; anything which showed disregard for *tambu*, the rules for correct living.

Being responsible for good relations between the living and the dead, priests, like the ancestors, were the moral guardians of their own small communities. It was they who kept the peace and preserved harmony by maintaining the *tambus* backed by the power of their ancestors. The most important priests in particular were so *tambu* themselves that they could not even eat food prepared by women, and their everyday lives were surrounded by restrictions to make them acceptable to the ancestors.

Quarrels and feuds

However, people did not respect *tambus* solely out of fear of the ancestors or respect for their priests, particularly when it came to offending other people's ancestors, who reacted against their own descendants. When it came to offences by distant relatives of other neighbourhoods, men were inclined to take matters into their own hands. They might turn to magic, for instance by taking a person's leftover food and putting it with danger-ous substances to make them ill. This was the secret way: it would be difficult to prove if anyone had actually done it. More often people de-manded compensation in shell money from those who had wronged them. Any wrong could be paid for in this way, from pigs damaging a garden to killing, but men often had to be prepared to back up their demands by violence. Some of the most serious quarrels arose over the strict code of sexual morals. If a man seduced another's wife or daughter, he was likely to be killed by her menfolk if discovered, unless his relatives could nego-tiate a very large compensation payment or arrange for the couple to marry, if they were single. Women were *tambu* too, in the sense that their chastity must be respected.

Playing the
panpipes for a
dance.

In the past there was always the danger that quarrels over women, over pig-stealing or land ownership and other matters would lead to bloodshed. Men who could not obtain the compensation they thought they deserved, or were too angry even to ask for it, might try to kill the offender or one of his relatives. Alternatively they might offer a large reward for a skilled fighter to do it for them. Men who made a speciality of collecting these rewards often became wealthy and powerful leaders, establishing fearful reputations for themselves. When a person was killed his relatives in turn would have someone else killed in revenge and the feud might go on for years. This state of affairs often made it dangerous for people to travel far outside their own neighbourhoods. Men always carried arms wherever they went: clubs, spears, or bows and arrows, or guns and bush knives obtained in trade. Feasts and market days could be tense occasions when men tried to settle old scores.

Changing times

Being accustomed to settle their own disputes and quarrels by force, the Kwara'ae, like other Malaitans, tried at first to settle their differences with outsiders in the same way. Their early experiences of Europeans were often far from agreeable and for many years Malaita was a dangerous place for visitors.

Although Europeans began to visit the Solomon Islands regularly early in the nineteenth century, it was not until the 1860s that they started to show much interest in the islands. Then they began to seek cheap labour for the plantations they were establishing, first in Fiji and then in Queensland. Ships began to tour the islands picking up and returning men on contracts to work for a few years abroad. Malaita, with its large population, was an important source of labour. Many volunteered for the sake of adventure and the trade goods they could obtain for their wages; some were kidnapped or taken under false pretences. The recruiters were often unscrupulous and the work poorly paid under harsh conditions. Malaitans resented mistreatment and frequently avenged themselves by massacring the crews of visiting ships, while the British Navy retaliated by bombarding villages nearby. By the early twentieth century, when the Queensland labour trade was stopped and the British had officially taken over the islands, Malaita had a wicked reputation among Europeans in the Pacific.

By this time the experience of working for Europeans had created a lasting impression on some Malaitan men, and a few began to live as Christians on their return home, backed by Australian and British missions. By the 1920s the British colonial government had subdued the leading fighters and stopped revenge killings, and Malaitans were more or less at peace with one another and with Europeans. The British started setting up their own 'headmen' as local leaders to enforce colonial laws and collect taxes. As time went on traditional leaders, priests, wealthy men and fighters, lost much of their authority in their own communities. Malaitans continued to work abroad, now in other islands in the Solomons, and they

became more and more involved in the European plantation economy which was developing there. Life on Malaita was changing rapidly and people began to seek ways of adjusting to the new circumstances. For some the benefits of their ancestors' power seemed less important than before, especially when dealing with new conditions of life under the British. As missions became more active around the islands, Christianity seemed to more and more people to offer a solution: a new way of life with new opportunities to benefit from the changing times.

The way Christianity was presented by the early European missionaries did indeed make it seem like a new way of life. Most missionaries were intolerant of any local traditions which conflicted with European customs and today, when most Solomon Islanders run their own churches, many of them share the early missionaries' opinions. The missionaries regarded the ancestors as agents of Satan (*devols* as they are called in pijin today). Converts had to abandon their ancestors, desecrate their shrines and abolish sacrifices, rituals and *tambus*. Of course this made it impossible for Christians to live with everyone else and in the early years they lived in isolated communities on the coasts. The fundamentalist churches to which most Christian Kwara'ae belong also oppose or restrict other traditional practices from feasting and bridewealth gifts to traditional singing, dancing and costume, all regarded as 'heathen'.

These changes evidently appealed to many people seeking a new way of life, and in any case they were conditions which had to be accepted by those seeking the benefits of Christianity. Over the years more and more people left their scattered hamlets in the hills and moved to larger villages nearer the coasts. Here they received education, or at least basic literacy, and Bible teaching, and they have gained better opportunities for trade and government services from the ships which travel the islands. Equally important, with God to protect and aid them they felt themselves freed from the authority of their ancestors. God does not demand costly sacrifices or impose complex rules about defilement. Christians only have to attend church regularly and lead good lives according to the same basic moral rules which the Kwara'ae have always believed in, and few expect God to punish them if they stray. On the other hand the ancestors still have power over those who choose to worship them. Both Christians and those who follow the traditional way of life believe in one another's religions: it is simply a matter of which they choose to follow.

Schools, started by the missions, are an important part of the Christian way of life.

Colonialism and *custom*

Of all areas on the main island of Malaita Kwara'ae has been most affected by colonial changes, being accessible from good harbours in the east and west and having less of the remote and rugged mountainous country where people in other parts of Malaita still lead relatively isolated lives. By the Second World War, the majority of Kwara'ae were Christians. However, like other Malaitans they continued to resent the way that Europeans had taken over their country, forcing new laws upon them, taxing them while paying poor wages and generally treating them as inferiors. They felt they were no longer in control of their own lives, and that they were losing

Local stores sell a variety of manufactured goods. This one is larger than most.

their old traditions of *custom* without getting their fair share of the benefits brought by new developments on the islands. The events of the Second World War gave them an opportunity to change all this. Encouraged by the collapse of the British administration when the Japanese invaded Guadalcanal and by the wealth and generosity of the Americans who took over in their turn, Malaitans devised their own alternative to the colonial government. In 1944 they set up their own administration, known as 'Marching Rule', and by a remarkable feat of organisation they united the whole island under a system of 'chiefs' and officials. People moved into towns around the coasts, with communal farms, their own taxation, police and courts.

Marching Rule was intended to free the people from foreign control and enable them to adapt colonial development to the *custom* they chose to preserve. Malaitans refused to co-operate with the British administration or European businesses, demanding better wages and education and recognition of their own system of local government. They appealed to their ancestors or to God to support their cause. The British reacted by imprisoning hundreds of people, before meeting some of their demands and giving them their own elected island Council.

Since the time of Marching Rule the Kwara'ae way of life has continued to change. Many people stayed in the coastal districts and more and more have become involved in small businesses of various kinds. Some have coconut plantations, others raise cattle or operate small stores selling manufactured goods, and transport has improved with new motor roads across the island. Many continue to work abroad from time to time and large numbers of Kwara'ae now live and work at Honiara, the Solomon Islands' capital on Guadalcanal, which has many of the facilities of a European-style town. Education is improving and most young men are

15

literate, while some now have skilled jobs in government and business. By contrast there are still perhaps a hundred people following the traditional religion who live much as their ancestors did half a century ago.

The majority of Kwara'ae combine self-sufficiency with a desire for whatever Western facilities and manufactured goods they can afford. However, they still face problems in maintaining their cherished *custom* at the same time. Many people are disturbed at the way new agricultural developments threaten the traditional inheritance of land, at the decline in sexual morality and bridewealth gifts and the problems of enforcing proper penalties for wrong-doing. Even now that the Solomon Islands are an independent country some still feel they do not have enough control of their own affairs. Those who are most concerned continue the work started in Marching Rule, writing down the genealogies which proclaim everyone's rights to their land, and trying to standardise those *tambus* which they wish to incorporate into government law. Their aim is to unite the Kwara'ae as descendants of the original ancestor in the story under their own leaders, successors to the priests of old, who they now call 'tribal chiefs' and 'paramount chiefs'. Some Kwara'ae still desire freedom from any government, and have founded a new church which recognises no authority but God.

As Christians most Kwara'ae want the *custom* they follow to be Christian too. It is often said that the first ancestor in the story worshipped God, that the *tambu* rules which he brought were in the form of ten commandments, and that the traditional religion of his descendants was like that of the Old Testament. Like the colonial developments of which it is a part, the Kwara'ae have tried to make Christianity their own, so that their religion continues to uphold the ancient traditions of *custom* and self-determination which they value so much.

(Right) Paramount Chief Osifera in his *custom* house, a museum and meeting house where the staff of the first ancestor is kept.

(Cover) Tea is one of the imported luxuries much appreciated by Kwara'ae today.

Further reading

Little has been written about the Kwara'ae, but available books on other Malaitan peoples include:

Hogbin, I. *Experiments in Civilisation* (London, 1939, reprinted 1969)

Keesing, R. *'Elota's Story: the Life and Times of a Solomon Islands Big Man* (Queensland, 1978)

Other books may be consulted in the Museum of Mankind Reference Library.

Photographs taken in East Kwara'ae, 1979, by Ben Burt

© 1981   The Trustees of the British Museum

Published by British Museum Publications Limited
6 Bedford Square, London WC1B 3RA

ISBN   0-7141-1565-7

Printed in England by Saffron Press Limited, Saffron Walden, Essex